SPIDERS AROUND THE WORLD

All About North American CELLAR SPIDERS

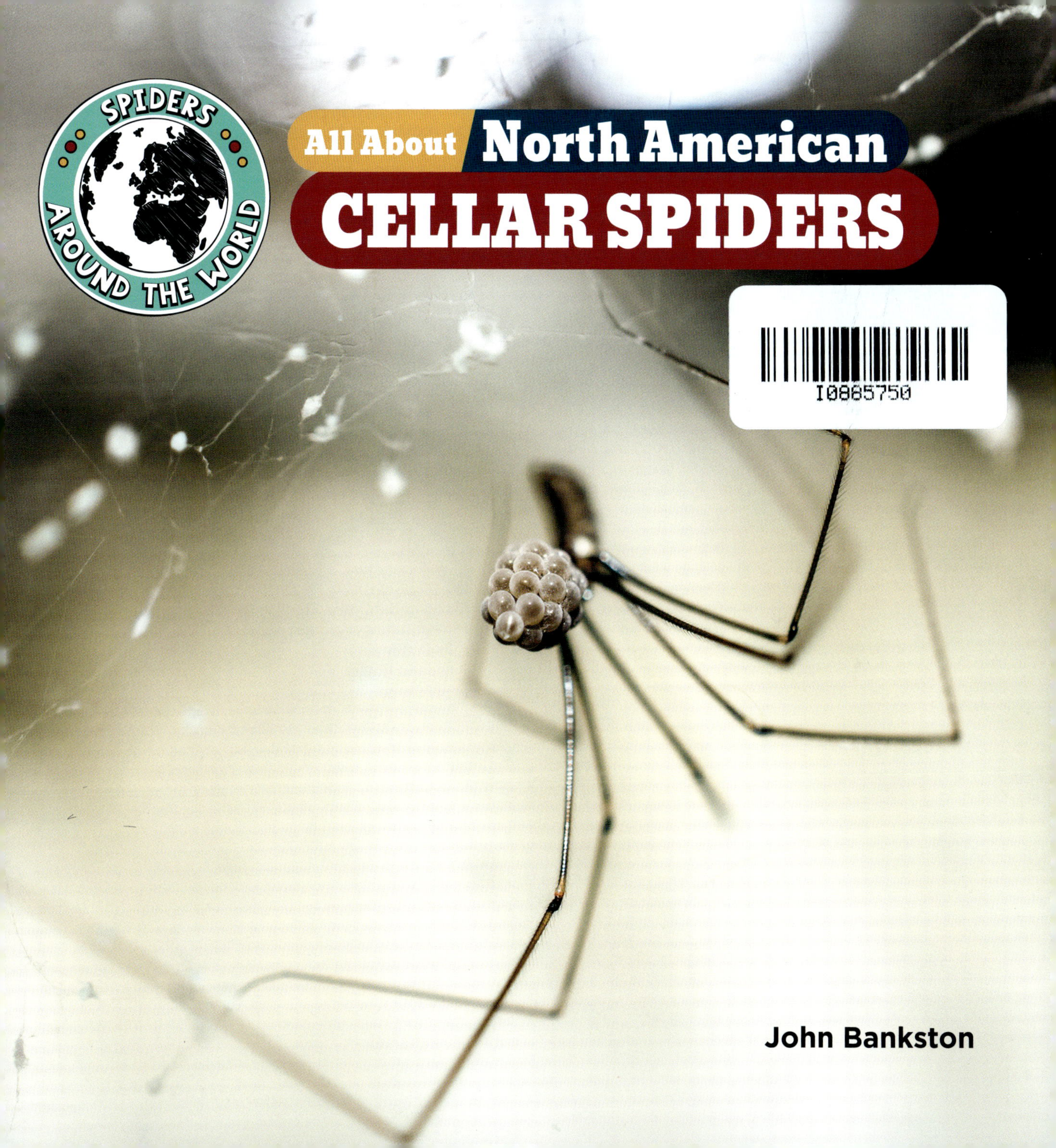

John Bankston

Mitchell Lane
PUBLISHERS
2001 SW 31st Avenue
Hallandale, FL 33009
www.mitchelllanepub.com

Little Mitchie

First Edition, 2025.

Author: John Bankston
Designer: Ed Morgan
Editor: Morgan Brody

Little Mitchie is an imprint of Mitchell Lane Publishers.

Title: All About North American Cellar Spiders
Description: Hallandale, FL : Mitchell Lane Publishers, [2025]

Series: Spiders Around the World: North America
Library bound ISBN: 978-1-68020-934-1
eBook ISBN: 978-1-68020-943-3
Paperback ISBN: 979-8-89260-161-0

Photo credits: cover, pp. 4-7, 12-21 Shutterstock; pp. 8-11 wikimedia

Contents

The cellar spider bounces on its web. The wolf spider approaches. It has great eyesight. The cellar spider bounces faster. This makes it hard to see.

Wolf spiders are twice as big as cellar spiders. Their **venom** is more powerful. So the cellar spider doesn't fight. It spins.

A web is spun over the wolf spider. It can't move. The cellar spider bites. Venom slowly kills the wolf spider. The cellar spider feeds and feeds.

Cellar spiders eat other spiders. Their **prey** also includes insects like flies or crickets. They really love ants. They are **nocturnal**—they come out at night. They hide during the day. You'll find them in piles of wood. They also enjoy old clothes.

The body of a cellar spider is smaller than a pencil's eraser. Their legs are three times that size! Hairs on their legs warn them when prey is near.

Cellar spiders can be gray, tan, or white. They are good at blending in. This is called **camouflage**.

Females lay egg sacs with 50 eggs inside. Egg sacs look like a clear berry. Mother cellar spiders carry the sacs in their mouths.

Newborn **spiderlings** hold onto their moms. It takes them one year to become an adult.

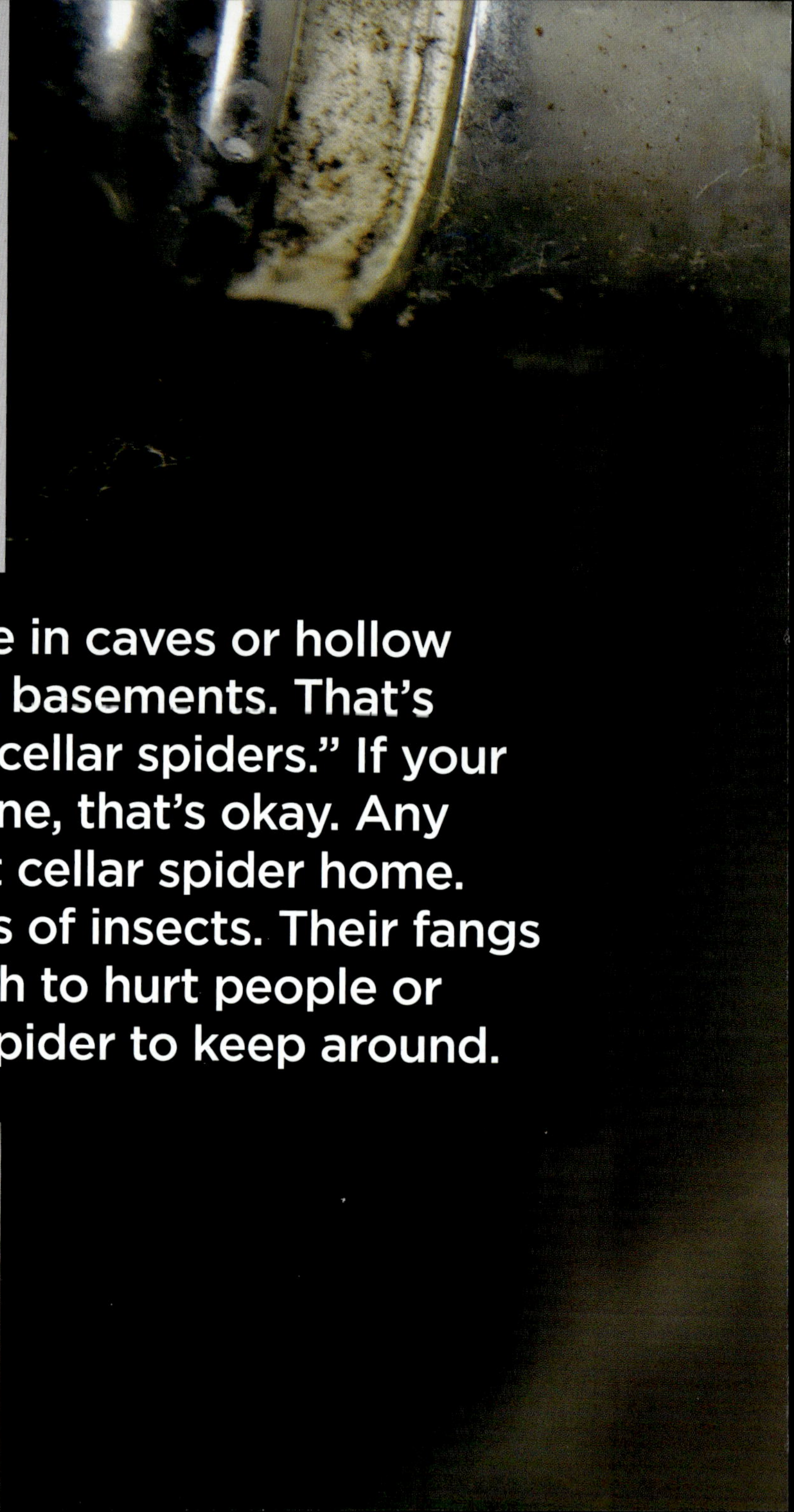

Cellar spiders can live in caves or hollow trees. They really like basements. That's why they are called "cellar spiders." If your home doesn't have one, that's okay. Any moist place is a great cellar spider home. These spiders eat lots of insects. Their fangs are not strong enough to hurt people or pets. This is a good spider to keep around.

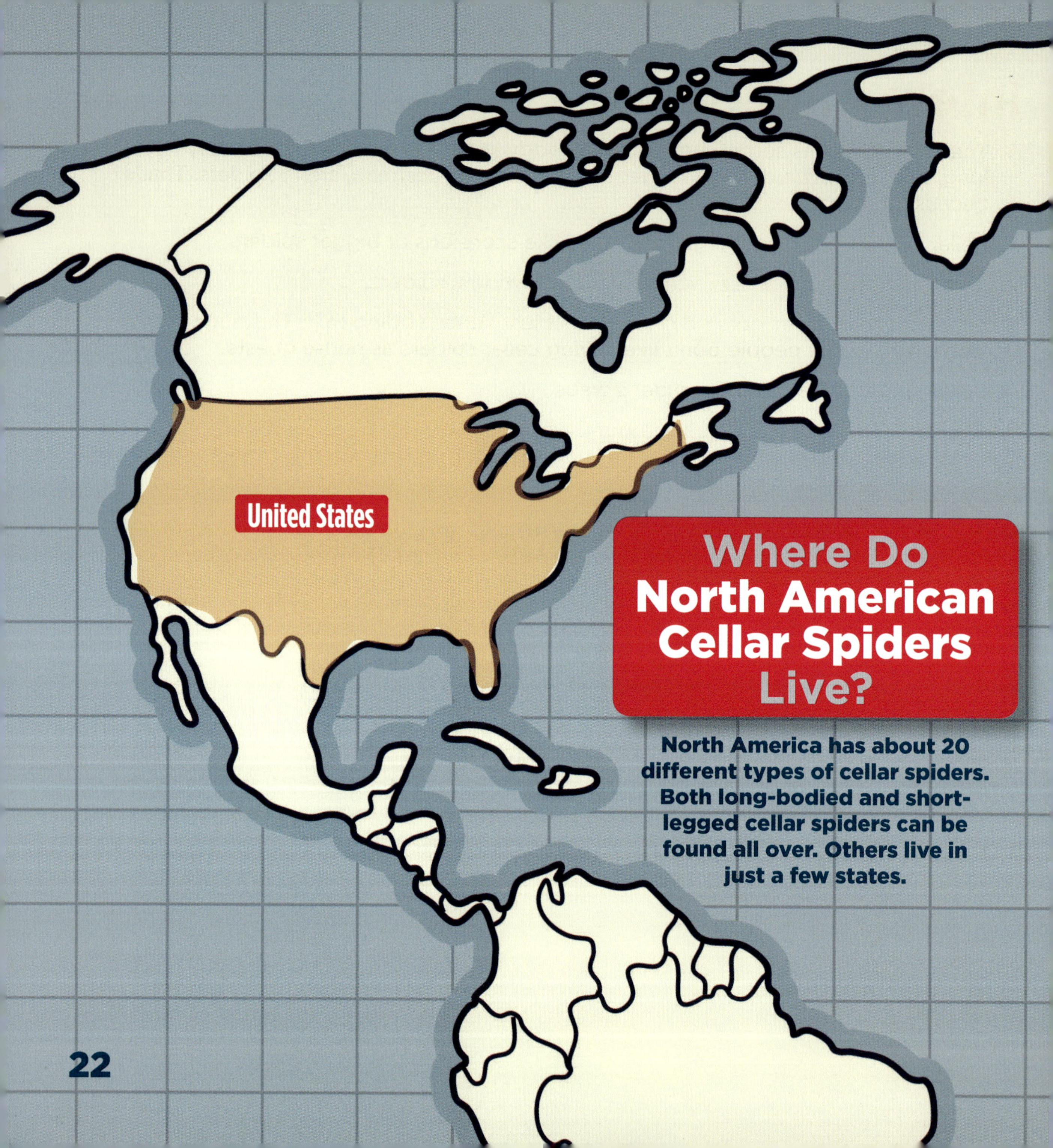

Where Do **North American Cellar Spiders** Live?

North America has about 20 different types of cellar spiders. Both long-bodied and short-legged cellar spiders can be found all over. Others live in just a few states.

Interesting Facts

- The cellar spider is sometimes called a daddy long legs spider because they have long, thin legs. True daddy long legs, also called harvestman, aren't spiders. That's because they can't make webs.
- Cellar spiders eat much larger creatures like scorpions or bigger spiders.
- Cellar spiders can eat very venomous black widow spiders.
- A cellar spider never gets rid of its web. It just keeps adding to it. This huge messy web is why some people don't like having cellar spiders as house guests.
- Cellar spiders invade other spider's webs.
- A cellar spider can wrap its silk around another spider six times a second.

Parts of a North American Cellar Spider

Spiders are **arachnids**. Arachnids have an exoskeleton. That means their skeleton is outside of their body. Their head and **thorax** are fused.

Abdomen
This is where the silk glands are. These are used to wrap prey and for web building. The heart and guts are also in the abdomen.

Eyes
Cellar spiders have eight eyes. There are three on each side of its head. Two more rest in the middle.

Legs
Like all arachnids they have eight legs, four on each side of the body. There are claws at the end. Their legs are very bendy.

Mouth
They have short fangs.

Glossary

arachnid **(a-rack-NID)**
An eight-legged creature without antenna

camouflage **(cam-O-flaj)**
When an animal blends in with its surroundings

nocturnal **(nok-TURN-al)**
Animals that are more active at night than in the day

prey **(pray)**
Insect or other creature hunted for food

spiderling **(spi-der-LING)**
A baby spider

thorax **(thor-AX)**
The middle part of the body

venom **(ven-OM)**
A dangerous liquid that is injected by an animal

Further Reading

London, Martha. *Spiders*. Newburyport, MA: Focus Readers, 2020.

Strattin, Lisa. *Facts About the Cellar Spider.* (A Picture Book For Kids), 2022.

All Things Spiders For Kids: Filled With Plenty of Facts, Photos, and Fun to Learn all About Spiders. Berlin, Germany: Admore Publishing, 2022.

On the Internet

Find out more from The Critter Catalog: " Pholcidae (Cellar Spiders)What do they look like?" University of Michigan. http://www.biokids.umich.edu/critters/Pholcidae/#:

Great Picture of a Long-Bodied Cellar Spider with its babies:
http://www.bio.brandeis.edu/fieldbio/heidi/pholicidaepholcus.html

Learn all about the Marbled Cellar Spider on Kidadl:
https://kidadl.com/facts/animals/marbled-cellar-spider-facts

Index